FIRST LIGHT TAROT

22 MAJORS 22 INSIGHTS 22 SPREAD CARDS

DINAH ROSEBERRY

4880 Lower Valley Road • Atglen, PA 19310

Other Schiffer Books by the Author:

Ghosts of Valley Forge and Phoenixville
ISBN: 978-0-7643-2633-2

Cape May Haunts (with Laurie Hull)
ISBN: 978-0-7643-2821-3

Spooky York, Pennsylvania (with Scott Butcher)
ISBN: 978-0-7643-3021-6

Spooky Creepy Baltimore County
ISBN: 978-0-7643-3254-8

Psychic Pets: Solving Paranormal Mysteries
ISBN: 978-0-7643-3398-9

Ghost Hunters' Tool Kit (with Stuart Schneider)
ISBN: 978-0-7643-3912-7

Animals Impacting the World (with Mary Gasparo)
ISBN: 978-0-7643-4237-0

UFO and Alien Management: A Guide to Discovering, Evaluating, and Directing Sightings, Abductions, and Contactee Experiences
ISBN: 978-0-7643-4606-4,

Copyright © 2016 by
Schiffer Publishing (Dinah Roseberry)

Library of Congress
Control Number: 2015949990

All rights reserved. No part of this work may be reproduced or used in any form or by any means—graphic, electronic, or mechanical, including photocopying or information storage and retrieval systems—without written permission from the publisher.

The scanning, uploading, and distribution of this book or any part thereof via the Internet or via any other means without the permission of the publisher is illegal and punishable by law. Please purchase only authorized editions and do not participate in or encourage the electronic piracy of copyrighted materials. "Schiffer," "Schiffer Publishing, Ltd. & Design," and the "Design of pen and inkwell" are registered trademarks of Schiffer Publishing, Ltd.

Designed by Justin Watkinson
Type set in heading font/text font

ISBN: 978-0-7643-4573-9
Printed in China

Published by Schiffer Publishing, Ltd.
4880 Lower Valley Road
Atglen, PA 19310
Phone: (610) 593-1777; Fax: (610) 593-2002
E-mail: Info@schifferbooks.com

For our complete selection of fine books on this and related subjects, please visit our website at www.schifferbooks.com. You may also write for a free catalog.

This book may be purchased from the publisher. Please try your bookstore first.

We are always looking for people to write books on new and related subjects. If you have an idea for a book, please contact us at proposals@schifferbooks.com.

Schiffer Publishing's titles are available at special discounts for bulk purchases for sales promotions or premiums. Special editions, including personalized covers, corporate imprints, and excerpts can be created in large quantities for special needs. For more information, contact the publisher.

Images for the cards and book are courtesy of www.spacetelescope.org. See Author's Note.

For my mother, Hilda,
and my mother-in-law, Barbara

May the universe hold all the answers you seek.

ACKNOWLEDGMENTS

I'd like to acknowledge the people who "put up with" my constant ramblings about space, aliens, light beings, Greys, the paranormal, and writing-writing-writing (my author peers, family—(particularly my husband Carroll), friends, and my dogs—who will listen when all others are yawning with eyes glazed over . . . or asleep).

Always to Carolyn Giles, who believes in me through all the craziness and miles and time between us.

To the Lancaster Health System, with doctors (particularly Dr. Kerr), nurses, assistants, and a million others there who keep me healthy enough to continue the pursuit of my dreams through the most difficult times.

Thanks to all my cohorts working with this project at Schiffer, who often bring my world from disconnect to an end of model efficiency and beauty, then show it to the masses. Thanks to John Cheek for direction and Justin Watkinson for taking my love of a particular image and making it into a piece of artwork. To Catherine and Pete for standing with me on the project and Chris for taking it to the world.

"First light" is the moment a new telescope first opens itself up to the universe.

—The First Light Astronomy Club

CONTENTS

An Author's Note 12

Part I. 17
    This Deck's First Light 20
    Spreads 24
    Astrological Signs 30
    Numbers and
        Numerology 33
    Meditation 37
    The Images 38
    The Reading Process 40
    What You Can Expect
        from This Deck 41
    The Reference Card 42

Part II. 43
    The Majors 46
    0 Fool 48
    1 Magician 49
    2 High Priestess 50
    3 Empress 51
    4 Emperor 52
    5 Hierophant 53
    6 Lovers 54
    7 Chariot 55
    8 Strength 56
    9 Hermit 57
    10 Wheel of Fortune 58
    11 Justice 59
    12 Hanged Man 60
    13 Death 61
    14 Temperance 62
    15 Devil 63
    16 Tower 64
    17 Star 65
    18 Moon 66
    19 Sun 67
    20 Judgment 68
    21 World 69

Insight Cards 70
    1 Activate 72
    2 Attraction 73
    3 Battle 74
    4 Children 75
    5 Code 76
    6 Conspiracy 77
    7 Diversity 78
    8 Emotion 79
    9 Energy 80
    10 Harmony 81
    11 Healing 82
    12 Karma 83
    13 Messages 84
    14 Nature 85
    15 Portal 86
    16 Power 87
    17 Resistance 88
    18 Soul Identity 89
    19 Source 90
    20 Thought 91
    21 Vibration 92
    22 Well Being 93

Part III 94
    Conclusion 95
    Bibliography 96

AN AUTHOR'S NOTE

Definition of "First Light" via www.definitions.net:
In astronomy, first light is the first use of a telescope to take an astronomical image after it has been constructed. This is often not the first viewing using the telescope; optical tests will probably have been performed during daylight to adjust the components . . . a first light is always a moment of great excitement, both for the people who designed and built the telescope, and for the astronomical community. . . . In physical cosmology, first light refers to the light emitted from the first generation of hyperstars, formed less than a billion years after the big bang, which brought to an end cosmological dark ages.

According to Hubble Telescope authorities:

Every ninety-seven minutes, Hubble completes a spin around Earth, moving at the speed of about five miles per second—fast enough to travel across the United States in about ten minutes. As it travels, Hubble's mirror captures light and directs it into its several science instruments.

The Hubble Telescope has been taking its round-about journey since 1990; you may not be able to imagine the varied and multitude of discoveries shot back to Earth via its mirrors in hopes that we might see what lies beyond. The Hubble Telescope's "eyes" have looked at phenomenal oddities outside our Earthly dwellings from thirteen to fourteen billion years ago, sending back information that has allowed scientists to look at evolution, dark energy, and other forces that lay persons may never ponder in often-mundane lives. Because of its scouting vision, we understand more than ever before how galaxies are formed, the strange gases and dusts that surround planet birthing grounds, intricacies about explosive energy, and much more.

To say that this telescope and those who work with it have thrust us into the future would be a simple statement that does not nearly delve into the connected sciences or concepts that will one day have all of us sitting on our own stars. That does not mean we would consider dismissing what we so often feel as "normal wear and tear, dude" when it comes to this massive undertaking and understanding of our scientific community. It's there for all of us—they are part of us. Still, we must give our best acknowledgments and regards to the people who inspire universal knowledge and a star chart for each and every individual as they go about their daily chores of discovering what needs knowing about the frontier of space.

Here then, first and foremost, I would like to acknowledge those formidable men and women on the first lines. Whether part of the Hubble team or their sidekick NASA, or any of the brilliant people from universities or private disciplines around the planet who interact, and study, and explore, we applaud you.

The images for this deck have many facets and those who have responsibility for their discovery, study, exploration, and presentation, are many. Without them, I would not have been able to intersect the universe with the individual divination as I've done here for the "good of the many" (thank you, Leonard Nimoy and *Star Trek* writers).

Within the guidebook, the cards have each been cropped so that a specific portion of the view will show. There are no other modifications. The box and book cover images have been created in the same manner and reflect works of art.

So, in what follows, I've noted each image by location name and give the distinguished credit to those involved:

Box: European Space Agency and Wolfram Freudling (Space Telescope-European Coordinating Facility/European Southern Observatory, Germany)

Guidebook cover: European Space Agency and Wolfram Freudling (Space Telescope-European Coordinating Facility/European Southern Observatory, Germany)

Front Matter, Parts & Miscellaneous Enhancements: NASA, ESA, and the Hubble Heritage Team (STScI/AURA). NASA, ESA, M. Livio and the Hubble 20th Anniversary Team (STScI), Acknowledgments: NASA/ESA. NASA, ESA, Martin Kornmesser (ESA/Hubble). NASA, ESA, CXC, and JPL-Caltech. X-ray: NASA/CXC/Univ. Potsdam/L. Oskinova et al.; Optical: ESA, NASA/STScI; Infrared: NASA/JPL-Caltech. NASA, Holland Ford (JHU), the ACS Science Team and ESA. NASA, ESA, the Hubble Heritage (STScI/AURA)-ESA/Hubble Collaboration, and W. Keel (University of Alabama).

Tarot Cards:

0 Fool: NASA, ESA and the Hubble Heritage Team STScI/AURA)-ESA/Hubble Collaboration

1 Magician: European Space Agency and Wolfram Freudling (Space Telescope-European Coordinating Facility/European Southern Observatory, Germany)

2 High Priestess: ESA/NASA, the AVO project and Paolo Padovani

3 Empress: NASA, ESA, and the Hubble Heritage Team (STScI/AURA). Acknowledgment: J. Hughes (Rutgers University)

4 Emperor: NASA, Holland Ford (JHU), the ACS Science Team and ESA

5 Hierophant: A. Schaller (STScI)

6 Lovers: NASA, ESA and the Hubble SM4 ERO Team

7 Chariot: NASA, Holland Ford (JHU), the ACS Science Team and ESA

8 Strength: NASA, ESA/Hubble and the Hubble Heritage Team

9 Hermit: NASA, ESA, and G. Bacon (Space Telescope Science Institute)

10 Wheel of Fortune: NASA, ESA, and the Hubble Heritage Team (STScI/AURA)

11 Justice: NASA/ESA and The Hubble Heritage Team (STScI/AURA)

12 Hanged Man: NASA, ESA, and The Hubble Heritage Team STScI/AURA)

13 Death: NASA, ESA, and G. Bacon (STScI)

14 Temperance: NASA, ESA and the Hubble Heritage Team (STScI/AURA)

15 Devil: NASA, ESA, and the Hubble Heritage Team (AURA/STScI)

16 Tower: NASA, ESA, M. Robberto (Space Telescope Science Institute/ESA) and the Hubble Space Telescope Orion Treasury Project Team

17 Star: NASA, ESA and P. Kalas (University of California, Berkeley, USA)

18 Moon: Lick Observatory

19 Sun: NASA, ESA, L. Calçada

20 Judgment: NASA, ESA and Allison Loll/Jeff Hester (Arizona State University). Acknowledgment: Davide De Martin (ESA/Hubble)

21 World: NASA, ESA, S. Beckwith (STScI) and the Hubble Heritage Team (STScI/AURA)

Insight Cards:
Insight 1: NASA, ESA and the Hubble Heritage Team (STScI/AURA)

Insight 2: ESA/Hubble & NASA. Acknowledgment: Luca Limatola

Insight 3: ESA/Hubble & NASA

Insight 4: X-ray: NASA/CXC/Univ. Potsdam/L. Oskinova et al.; Optical: ESA, NASA/STScI; Infrared: NASA/JPL-Caltech

Insight 5: NASA, ESA, E. Sabbi (STScI)

Insight 6: NASA & ESA

Insight 7: ESA, NASA

Insight 8: NASA, ESA, the Hubble Heritage Team (STScI/AURA), A. Nota (ESA/STScI), and the Westerlund 2 Science Team

Insight 9: NASA, ESA and Jesús Maíz Apellániz (Instituto de Astrofísica de Andalucía, Spain). Acknowledgment: Davide De Martin (ESA/Hubble)

Insight 10: NASA, ESA, M. Regan and B. Whitmore (STScI) and R. Chandar (University of Toledo, USA)

Insight 11: NASA, ESA, and the Hubble Heritage STScI/AURA)-ESA/Hubble Collaboration. Acknowledgment: Robert A. Fesen (Dartmouth College, USA) and James Long (ESA/Hubble)

Insight 12: NASA, ESA, the Hubble Heritage (STScI/AURA)-ESA/Hubble Collaboration, and the Digitized Sky Survey 2. Acknowledgment: J. Hester (Arizona State University) and Davide De Martin (ESA/Hubble)

Insight 13: NASA, ESA, and the Hubble Heritage Team (STScI/AURA) Acknowledgment: W. Blair (Johns Hopkins University)

Insight 14: NASA/ESA and The Hubble Heritage Team STScI/AURA)

Insight 15: NASA, ESA, D. Coe, G. Bacon (STScI)

Insight 16: Hui Yang (University of Illinois) and NASA/ESA

Insight 17: NASA, ESA, and G. Bacon (STScI)

Insight 18: NASA, ESA, the Hubble Heritage Team (STScI/AURA), A. Nota (ESA/STScI), and the Westerlund 2 Science Team

Insight 19: NASA, ESA, Harald Ebeling (University of Hawaii at Manoa) & Jean-Paul Kneib (LAM)

Insight 20: NASA, ESA, M. Montes (IAC), and J. Lotz, M. Mountain, A. Koekemoer, and the HFF Team (STScI)

Insight 21: NASA, ESA, Q. D. Wang (Univ. of Massachusetts, Amherst, USA) and STScI

Insight 22: NASA, ESA, SSC, CXC and STScI

Spread Cards:
1. NASA, ESA, the Hubble Heritage Team (STScI/AURA), and R. Gendler (for the Hubble Heritage Team). Acknowledgment: J. GaBany

2. NASA, ESA

3. NASA, ESA, N. Smith (University of California, Berkeley), and The Hubble Heritage Team (STScI/AURA)

4. NASA, ESA, and the Hubble Heritage Team (STScI/AURA)

5. NASA, ESA, and Johan Richard (Caltech, USA) Acknowledgment: Davide De Martin & James Long (ESA/Hubble)

6. NASA, ESA and Jesús Maíz Apellániz (Instituto de Astrofísica de Andalucía, Spain)

7. NASA, ESA, ESO, D. Lennon and E. Sabbi (ESA/STScI), J. Anderson, S. E. de Mink, R. van der Marel, T. Sohn, and N. Walborn (STScI), N. Bastian (Excellence Cluster, Munich), L. Bedin (INAF, Padua), E. Bressert (ESO), P. Crowther (Sheffield), A. de Koter (Amsterdam), C. Evans (UKATC/STFC, Edinburgh), A. Herrero (IAC, Tenerife), N. Langer (AifA, Bonn), I. Platais (JHU) and H. Sana (Amsterdam)

8. NASA, ESA, A. Aloisi (STScI/ESA), and The Hubble Heritage (STScI/AURA)-ESA/Hubble Collaboration

9. ESA/Hubble & NASA

10. NASA, ESA

11. NASA, Holland Ford (JHU), the ACS Science Team and ESA

12. NASA, ESA, C. R. O'Dell (Rice University), and S. K. Wong (Rice University)

13. NASA, ESA, the Hubble Heritage Team (STScI/AURA), A. Nota (ESA/STScI), and the Westerlund 2 Science Team

14. NASA, ESA, M. Robberto (Space Telescope Science Institute/ESA) and the Hubble Space Telescope Orion Treasury Project Team

15. NASA, ESA, E. Sabbi (STScI)

16. NASA, ESA and Q. D. Wang (University of Massachusetts, Amherst)

17. NASA, ESA, M. Robberto (Space Telescope Science Institute/ESA) and the Hubble Space Telescope Orion Treasury Project Team

18. NASA/ESA, N. Walborn and J. Mamz-Apellaniz (Space Telescope Science Institute, Baltimore, MD), R. Barba (La Plata Observatory, La Plata, Argentina)

19. ESO. Acknowledgments: J. Alves (Calar Alto, Spain), B. Vandame, and Y. Beletski (ESO). Processing by B. Fosbury (ST-ECF)

20. NASA, ESA

21. N. Smith and NOAO/AURA/NSF

22. Davide De Martin (ESA/Hubble), the ESA/ESO/NASA Photoshop FITS Liberator & Digitized Sky Survey 2

Card Backs: ESA/Hubble & NASA Acknowledgement: Gilles Chapdelaine. NASA, ESA and H. Richer (University of British Columbia). NASA, ESA.

Back Matter:
Conclusion: NASA, ESA, Martin Kornmesser (ESA/Hubble)

HUBBLE SPACE EXPLORERS:
Your true dedication for paving the way to the stars cannot be understated.

PART I.

This Deck's First Light

"There's a time and a place for everything."

A quote like this can be heard coming from my mouth any number of times when things seem to begin with a wide chasm and then quickly (and mostly surprisingly) move into a narrow path that dumps into an exact outcome and timeline newly desired. I'm still on the path as I write this on a Sunday afternoon in a small East Coast town in the United States and wondering where it will all lead—but I'm pretty sure that it will be heading out to the universe at "warp" speed sooner or later.

How does that happen? How does synchronicity start (possibly years before one can recognize it to be such), and then, seemingly overnight, produce something that connects people on continents, across oceans—all with varied borders and beliefs—and puts them into one small space in time to create something that has not, moments before, ever been imagined?

My path has been forking, and winding, and traveling up hills and down into meadows for some years now. I just hobble along as it goes, excited to learn the new lesson and never aware of a coming change until after it's happened and made the profound difference in my world. It started with ghost research, traipsing around haunted locations and using the new-fangled paranormal equipment as it was invented or repurposed to investigate the dead and the past. Then, at the same time, Tarot projects became part of my position at Schiffer Publishing, though I'd been reading the cards for some twenty-five years by the time I finally had the overnight realization that there was to be more to it than just my own readings of the cards. There were, of course, many tributaries during the years, but eventually, as I was researching the concept of raising vibrations, I was led to the stars . . . then on to the star beings (some call them aliens, others angels), UFOs, dimensions (other than our own) . . . to the people who needed help with these very things. An odd path? To be sure. But once I began channeling Light Beings and saw a display of UFOs (along with two other investigators) that was so startling that I knew a change was coming . . . well, I knew that the path I was on was the correct one for me. The hard part (and this is probably true for everyone) was staying the course.

First Light began as a traditional Tarot concept, but within minutes (it would feel), it changed into something much more. Though I was aware of the importance of the Major Arcana cards, the "knowing" was given that rather than providing Minors (the pip cards), I was to give the advice directly affecting humanity's everyday experience via those from worlds beyond. I was to interpret "vibrations."

"Vibrations are the basis of all life," the Light Beings told me. We are each made of the energy that, when connected, becomes vibrations that run the world, that connect the masses—or in contrast, ruin or destroy the world and stimulate negativity for the masses. There is only the availability of choice—and hopefully that choice will be for each person to live well. One set of vibrations can bring or send a person along a wonderful path of self-discovery and a magnitude of understanding and success. The wrong path . . . well, the basic guidance is: don't go there, don't think about that, don't draw negative vibration to you. But how does this work? I wondered, *can we be of sound mind enough to keep off that negative, vibrating path?* This wasn't just a decision to drink the Appletini or choose skim milk, but rather it led to highly shared conditions: political, religious, and contexts of every other issue facing every single person alive every single day. It's not easy to stay positive all the time. It's not normal to think "outward" instead of "inward," but I was willing to listen to the advice from these beings who seemed to have all the answers. "What," they said, "would you do if you had a system to assist you in making the correct determinations? What if the advice given touched your very soul—and the soul of every other person as well? What if there was support in navigating daily turmoil and to help you take the 'high road?' And what if it was so easy to use that people could not help but love it?"

Impossible. (Yup, there's the negativity coming out. Everyone has it at one time or another.) They just chuckled in my head. (Could this be hysteria? . . . Nah . . . well, maybe.) I was directed to work with a card deck—something I was comfortable with—to provide a simple way to connect the Light Beings, the stars, and the universe to each of us. Oh, make no mistake, my first thought was: Gee, I work with these things every day and there are hundreds of card systems that offer assistance to the hardworking self. They nodded in my mind's eye. "Yes," they advised, "but there is no connection to the stars or the universe in general for most of these. Each deck—even the ones that show the stars—is about connecting to the self. That is very important, but there is other advice that comes from beyond—ripe for the taking. Why wish on a star, when you can embrace one?"

So what is this deck to be today? Tarot? Yes. Oracle? Yes. Stars? Yes. Universal advice? Yes. Beautiful, thought-provoking images? Yes. Easy to use? Yes. The deck became a Tarot Majors deck with Insight cards encompassing all these things. It spoke of astrology and of numbers. The card names and descriptions were created to touch upon both human and universal topics. Therefore, the only credit I take is the uniting of the messages in this format to help lead humanity toward paths of love, light, and enlightenment—to raise vibrations. I was to offer a human interpretation just as if this were a traditional Tarot Major's deck for those who had that interest only for this moment in time, so you will find both upright and reversed explanations given for the Tarot cards. There is also an Insight interpretation, giving understanding to each individual's life and situation for those interested in looking beyond Earth's interior answers. Many readers will not need interpretation at all, because just as I have a connection to the cards and the stars, readers, too, will feel that association. I have also pulled in the twelve astrological signs to help with personality identification, conflict resolution, and a greater awareness of how the Tarot incorporates the signs of our lives. Through the Insights, I touch on numerology, presenting a method to find what concept you should work on throughout a day, a situation, or a specific other occurrence or timeframe. Explanations for finding your lucky number(s) are also offered.

This deck can be used in several ways.

- The cards can be used as a traditional Tarot Major's deck with 22 cards, without using the Insight guidance cards, as you look inward to the self.

- The Insight cards can be used as a standalone oracle deck that provides wisdom from beyond our Earth, taking into consideration those who can look outward.

- The cards can be used as a traditional Tarot Major's deck with the 22 Insight cards being used as clarifiers in a traditional spread, or they can be shuffled right into the deck and used as part of the spread. All spreads accommodating 44 cards will work well with this deck if you already have a favorite.

- Many people like to pull a card each day for guidance. That can be done as well, and if you choose, you can pull one Major and one Insight card each day for direction— or one a week or one a month . . . .

- Readers may find specific focus for readings or lucky numbers.

- Astrological signs will give insight to connections to Tarot cards and the people/personalities who may be involved in the readings.

- There is a special spread called the Universal Spread to help deliver the messages you require for your situations (just in case you want one!).

- The Insight cards and the spread cards can be used with any other Tarot or oracle deck.

- Meditation upon any of the celestial images can be instituted.

Spreads

An explanation about spreads is important as this is a new and fun concept. Most divination decks require you to learn spreads or copy them to gain the advice you need. This takes time and mostly involves open books until your memory holds. Here, there are twenty-two spread cards provided that give you card placement without you ever having to lay them in crosses, or circles, or lines, or any pattern at all. They come pre-marked for top most-asked questions and issues that people desire during readings. Just look through the spread cards to consider their topics and choose the ones you'd like to include in your reading! All of them? Fine. One of them. Yes. Three? Of course. Lay them down in any way that suits you. Then once you shuffle the Tarot and Insight cards in the deck, place a card (either a Tarot, Insight, or any combination of cards) on top of each spread card. The spread card gives you the prompt for that particular Tarot or Insight card's message.

For example, one of the spread cards you might choose is "Present." When you lay down a shuffled Tarot or Insight card on top of the card labeled "Present," the card on top will be offering a message about what is happening in the present. To further illustrate:

TIPS

Consider the amount of space you have to lay out a reading. The cards are large and big spreads take a lot of space! With too little space to see the cards, it's easy to miss important connections. I find this problem to be stressful. This would not be as big a problem for a three-card spread, but when you choose above five headings...well, readings can become difficult.

It is best to start out with three to five cards, rather than using larger numbers of cards or the entire offering. You will find that this system gives very complex readings and since they are chosen by the querent (who may not always be the reader), having too much information at one time can cause great duress because linking topics becomes complicated. Once you become proficient, add cards as you feel ready.

Though the idea is for the person being read to choose the spread cards they want, it often helps in the beginning for the reader to choose the Past, Present, and Furture cards to begin and thereby ask that the querent only contribute two or three cards to the layout. This is a way to teach your mind slowly to work outside of any Tarot methods you've used in the past. If you've read the Tarot before, you know that there are some cards that seem important in the reading above all others and give you a headstart to your reading. Controlling just a couple cards will allow you a grace period for understanding movement outside the usual layouts. And truth be told, you may not want to give up any control of cards ever. You could easily do all the choosing yourself! Start with five to ten cards because otherwise the story becomes very complex. The better you get, the more cards you can add.

SPREAD CARD: Present
Card pulled from the shuffled deck: 0 Fool

This coupling would tell you that in the **present**, you are about to embark on a journey, or possibly begin a new project. (This is where you go into the meaning of the Fool card.)

SPREAD CARD: Obstacle
Card pulled from the deck: 4 Emperor

The Emperor represents logic, so now to your Present, you've added an **Obstacle** card that reflects logic.

As an obstacle, it is possible that you are not looking at your new beginning logically—and that's a problem.

There are twenty possible spread cards preprinted, with two "Wild Cards" that you can assign any question or notation to.

Suppose you take one of the blank **Wild** spread cards and assign someone's name to it: Jane (a good friend of yours).

SPREAD CARD: Jane
Card pulled from the deck: 17 Resistance
(an Insight card)

So, you have a new beginning and a trip that you are not thinking logically about and now **Jane** is offering resistance to the plan.

Spread Cards

Each card you lay down will add to the story. As mentioned, there are twenty-two spread cards as follows:

1. Wild Card
2. Wild Card
3. Querent
4. Variables Affecting the Issue
5. Past
6. Recent Past
7. Near Future
8. Future
9. How Querent Sees Issue
10. Others Looking In
11. Personal Message
12. Outcome
13. Present
14. Why is This Happening?
15. First Step
16. What Should I Do?
17. When?
18. Strategy
19. Obstacles
20. Positive Surroundings
21. Who May Help?
22. Who May Hurt?

A Universal Spread

Some people will just want a preplanned spread just because they want one—and they should have it! So, I've included one for those who need more structure. Its card order is based loosely on the Celtic Cross spread and it does not utilize your new spread cards (but it would be very easy to insert any of the spread cards wherever you like into this one!). There is no specific way you need to lay down the cards for the Universal Spread, however, if you choose to use the Celtic Cross format, it may be easier to link cards that are close together as you would do in that process. Do note that the ten cards' placements do not correlate with the actual Celtic Cross. (You may use the traditional Celtic Cross—or any spread that you prefer—as long as you note what each placement means *before* you begin to read the cards.) That display, however, would look as follows:

1. Querent (Significator)
2. Situation from Earth Perspective
3. Star Being or Light Being View of the Situation
4. Obstacle according to the universe
5. The Strength that will most help the obstacle in card 4
6. Obstacle to finding the strength
7. The Strength that will most help the obstacle in card 6
8. Star Being or Light Being Advice
9. Likely Outcome
10. Word for the day to consider when stressed

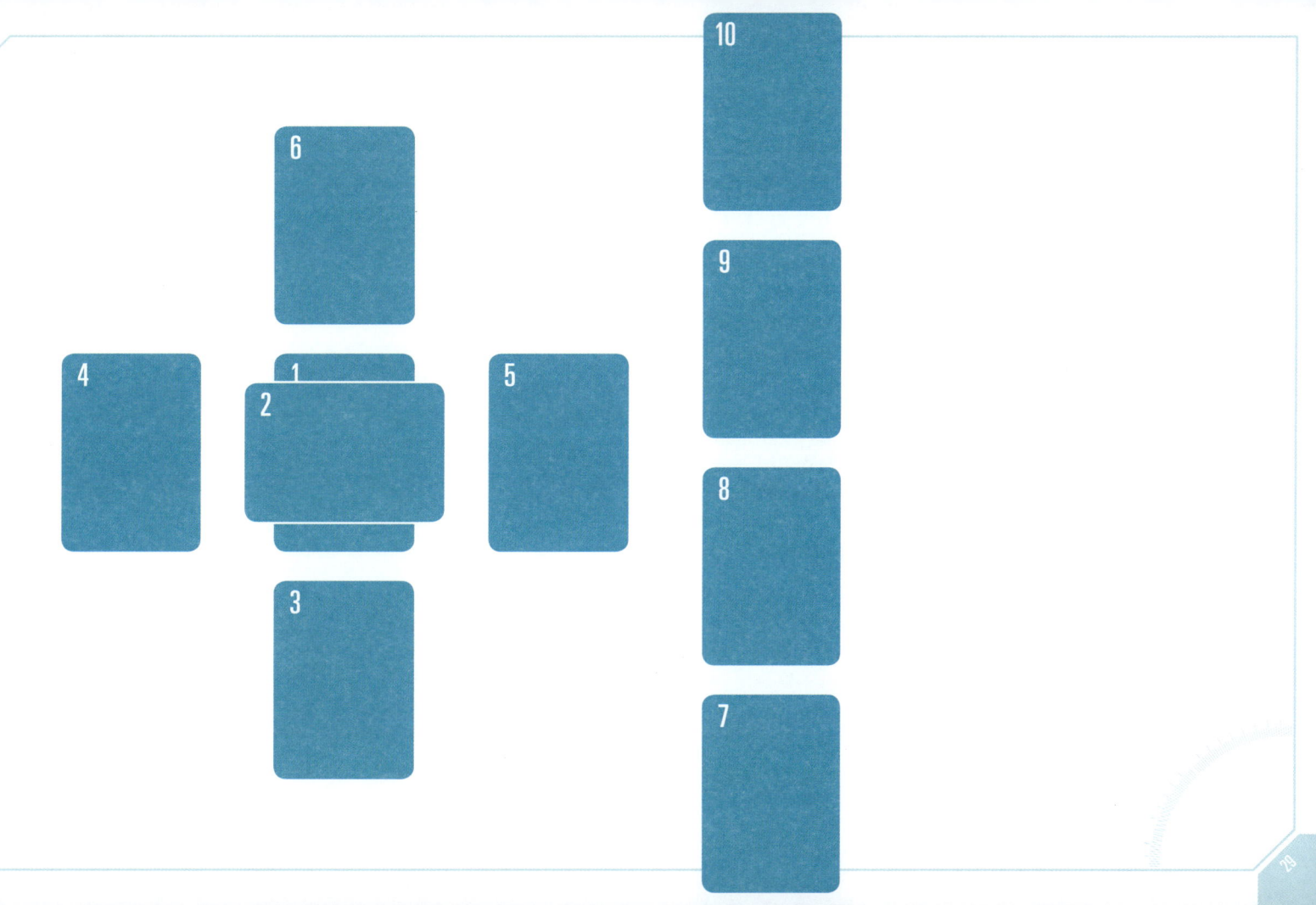

Astrological Signs

Each of the twelve astrological signs will be linked to a specific Major Arcana Tarot card, giving you insight into a personality that might be reflected for a specific location in the spread you've chosen to use. It could be your personality or another's, a focus on what tone of thinking should accompany the card's message, or a general feeling of the positive or negative personality traits around you at that moment that could escalate your situation to a conclusion.

More depth into a reading can be gleaned by studying astrological signs as their own specific topic and then adding that information to your arsenal of knowledge gained here. (Remember because there are only twelve signs, not all Major Arcana cards will be represented by astrological references.) These signs are marked on the appropriate cards for you to reference.

Astrological Identifiers for the Associated Majors

4 Emperor
Aries (March 21–April 19)
Takes chances, fast thinking, talented/
overbearing, easily convinced, aggressive

5 Hierophant
Taurus (April 20–May 20)
Dependable/
envious, obstinate

6 Lovers
Gemini (May 21–June 20)
Conversational, inquisitive/
spreads gossip, aggravating

7 Chariot
Cancer (June 21–July 22)
Sympathetic, reliable/
grumpy, defensive

8 Strength
Leo (July 23–August 22)
Flashy, likeable/
self-centered, controlling

9 Hermit
Virgo (Aug. 23–Sept. 22)
Intelligent, detail oriented/
controlling, self-important

11 Justice
Libra (September 23–October 22)
Creative, giving/
quarrelsome, sensitive

13 Death
Scorpio (October 23–November 21)
Hot-blooded, charismatic/
calculating, ruthless

14 Temperance
Sagittarius (November 22–Dececember 21)
Positive, distinctive/
reckless/haughty, rash

15 Devil
Capricorn (December 22–January 19)
Perrsistent/
negative, aggressive

17 Star
Aquarius (January 20–February 18)
Inspired, optimistic/
immature, inconsiderate

18 Moon
Pisces (February 19–March 20)
Creative, kindhearted/
impulsive, illogical

Using the prior spread example (under Spreads on page 25), the 4 Emperor card has the Aries astrological sign associated with it. Let's look at that information added to the rest of the reading:

SPREAD CARD: Present
Card pulled from the shuffled deck: 0 Fool

In the present, you are about to embark on a journey, or possibly begin a new project.

SPREAD CARD: Obstacle
Card pulled from the deck: 4 Emperor

The Emperor represents logic. Adding the fact that the Emperor card is associated with someone who has Aries traits, you should consider that around this card is someone who takes chances, is a fast thinker, talented but possibly overbearing, easily convinced, but aggressive.

So, added to your Present, you've added an Obstacle card that reflects logic. As an obstacle, it is possible that you are not looking at your new beginning logically—and that's a problem. That problem could involve someone who thinks fast, is aggressive, etc.

WILD SPREAD CARD: Jane
Card pulled from the deck: 17 Resistance (an Insight card)

So, you have a new beginning and a trip that you are not thinking logically about, and there is someone (possibly you, but maybe Jane) who is taking chances. Jane is offering resistance to the plan.

The more cards you pull, the more the story will become more clear.

Numbers and Numerology

Each of the twenty-two Insight cards will have a number associated with it that will be shown on the card. Once your reading is completed, note the numbers shown on these cards (not including the number within the card's actual name), add them all together and then reduce them to their smallest form. The number you receive at the very end will be the concept that should be concentrated upon to give you successful results. It could be a warning, or simply the identification of a path to pursue. You will notice that when the cards reach 10, a two-digit number, these references will be reduced by adding one to the other (i.e. 1+0=1, therefore the number association for the number 10 would be 1. Number 11 would be 2, 1+1=2, and so on.

NUMBERS AND THEIR MEANINGS

1 — Male/yang, new starts, forging ahead, high energy

2 — Feminine/yin, the one in the middle (looking at all angles of a situation), tolerance and stamina

3 — Triangle, clarity, concentration, learn not to scatter energy

TIP

Sometimes it can be helpful to read the numbers as they come up without reducing them at the end of the reading into one number. There could be some reflection that might help when read individually. Feel free to do what you feel is best.

4 Down to earth, truthfulness, common sense, strength	**7** Solitude, in touch with nature, all kinds of cycles (life, death, growth), developing insight
5 Independence, flexibility, change, continuous movement	**8** Seeking answers, material into reality, control or responsibility in a field of interest, a focus on future
6 Harmony, intuition, balance, understanding	**9** Compassionate, patient, service to others, love, tolerance, forgiveness, high intelligence

In our sample reading we have so far:

> A new beginning and a trip that you are not thinking logically about, and there is someone (possibly you, but maybe Jane) who is taking chances. Jane is offering resistance to the plan.

The 17 Resistance card has a number association of 8 (1+7=8), which means: seeking answers, bringing the material into reality, control or responsibility in a field of interest, a focus on future.

So the concept that you should be concentrating upon in this reading would be that of seeking responsible answers for your future. Maybe you should be researching this journey a bit more before you hop into something that might not be right for you. The full reading then for these 3 cards would be:

> A new beginning and a trip that you are not thinking logically about, and there is someone (possibly you, but maybe Jane) who is taking chances. Jane is offering resistance to the plan. More research is needed. Figure out whether you are headed down the right path before starting.

Meditation

Practicing meditation is an important part of getting to know both the inner and outer self. By focusing on something that "speaks to you," meditation can take you away from your daily comings and goings by centering your very being.

To use *First Light* as a device for meditation, merely look through the cards to see which image resonates with you each time you meditate. (You need not use the same card all the time.) You could look at the card's meaning and incorporate that information, but that is not really necessary. Just the image alone can take you to worlds beyond and assist you with the important task of learning to raise your vibration.

Merely find a quiet place without distractions, light a candle if you choose (this too is optional), prop up a card image you are drawn to within easy sight, and begin with a regiment of slow breathing, counting your breaths and concentrating on them. Once your body has slowed and you feel relaxed, begin looking deep into the image. Your vision will start to glaze over as you start to see things you'd not seen before. Trivial thoughts may enter your mind—feel free to just brush them away, or if you feel they are part of the meditation, let them flow from your mind into the image.

This is the time to ask questions of the universe. Answers will come immediately—the first thought that pops into your mind once you've asked a question will be your answer. Only positive affirming messages will be sent to you from the universe. It is likely that they will come to you in your own voice. Do not dismiss them or change them (as your mind may be prone to do).

When you finally decide to leave your meditation, open your eyes and then quickly write down the messages you've received. Drink water to hydrate.

> **TIP**
>
> Remember that you should only receive positive messages. Anything of a negative nature should be dismissed and your meditation halted. Your personal protection has not been conducted properly in this case. Never should you listen to a voice (even your own) that tells you to harm yourself or any other being of the world.

The Images

The beautiful photography for *First Light* comes to you from the Hubble Telescope. The far-reaching telescope orbits our Earth taking photographs of the universe that we live in. Astronomy has always been a study that brought forth great mysteries—sometimes solving them by taking that closer look, other times just creating more questions. This is why the Hubble images are so important to this deck and to your interpretation of the cards. Will their close proximity to your daily life situations be enhanced by an up-close and personal view, or will more mysterious things hamper or propel your movement forward? For Hubble, the scope just keeps on taking pictures, refining the images, and gallantly rushing toward clearer and clearer answers. While it draws light to dark energy, the identification of celestial bodies outside our realm, and tries to pinpoint the beginning of the universe, you will find yourself looking into the dark corners of the self, seeking the answers to unknown factors around you, and hoping to find the start of your journey to enlightenment by taking the self from that inward stance to the outer universal offerings. The bringing together of the telescope and the person then become quite copacetic.

Remember though, the Hubble has taken an enormous number of photos to help with that research. You are merely beginning and have much to learn, theories to spark or clarify, and details to bring to the light of day. There have been over 10,000 articles written by scientists about all manner of astronomical development based on Hubble images—so you can see that you are well behind the eight ball, or maybe loitering on the dark side of the moon. Either way, there's lots of work to do.

Each image chosen for this deck can take a reader deeper and deeper into a subconscious state when practicing divination or meditation (as mentioned earlier). Will the image have a meaning for you? This is an independent and personal question. Some will immediately gravitate toward a reasoning that correlates well with the card readings. Others will find that there is an extra added message that comes from the viewing of celestial bodies far away. Still others may not have a connection before using the deck for many months or years. This is something that will settle upon you when the time is right.

Many of these images came to me specifically as I looked at them for usage with a particular card. An example would be the Insight Card 4 Children—I see a child in that image, and I knew it was a card that wanted viewers to recognize all the aspects a child might have in a situation. Does a child fit figuratively into your path, are you behaving like a child, or are we all children moving toward enlightenment?

   A good indicator of how quickly you will find the images as part of your process will be the emotional response you had when you first chose to obtain this deck. What drew you and why? Give it thought and time. When you initially looked at the individual cards, which ones made you take in your breath?

The Reading Process

For whatever spread you plan for, once you have in mind what each card space will identify, shuffle the remaining ones, choosing either all forty-four cards, or you may separate them for either Tarot or Insight offerings. Lay a card down on top each of the spread cards you've picked (allowing the spread card identifier words to be visible to you) or in the fashion of any other spread you would like to use from other sources.

If you read a card and you need more information to understand the message, choose another card as a clarifier to lay on top of the first one and read the message combination. For example, if you were to choose the 2 High Priestess reversed and the message advises that there is deception around you and you are confused as to what that deception might be, you could pull a clarifying card to lay on top the first card to further advise you regarding what this deception involves. If that clarifying card was Insight 7 Diversity, mixing that message with the first one would give you clues to your deception. Possibly, this combination could mean that there is someone who does not respect you—or you them. Then move through the spread to receive further guidance. You can lay down a clarifying card on any card at any time. You can use as many as you choose. Or you can ask a question not related to the spread cards as an entirely new spread card (the wild card) to help you along.

First Light is an out-of-the-box system that can be used by anyone at all: experienced, first-timers, young and old, or by any religion (since there are no religious implications for any particular group). The universe has answers for all of us.

What You Can Expect from This Deck

There are many things you can accomplish with this deck. You could:

- Bring solutions for day-to-day situations to light
- Help to prepare long-term plans
- Interact with the universe
- Gain healing advice or inspiration
- Understand your place in the universe as a whole
- Figure out how to take action in your personal life
- Gain insight into the collective mind of those in the world around you
- Raise your vibration (the most important outcome)
- Find out how to read cards easily and without deep thought

The Reference Card

There is a quick and easy four-page reference card included that will help not only with the Tarot and Insight card keywords but also give you a quick glance at advice, astrological sign meanings, and numerology references for the appropriate cards. Keep this handy until you eventually know the cards by heart.

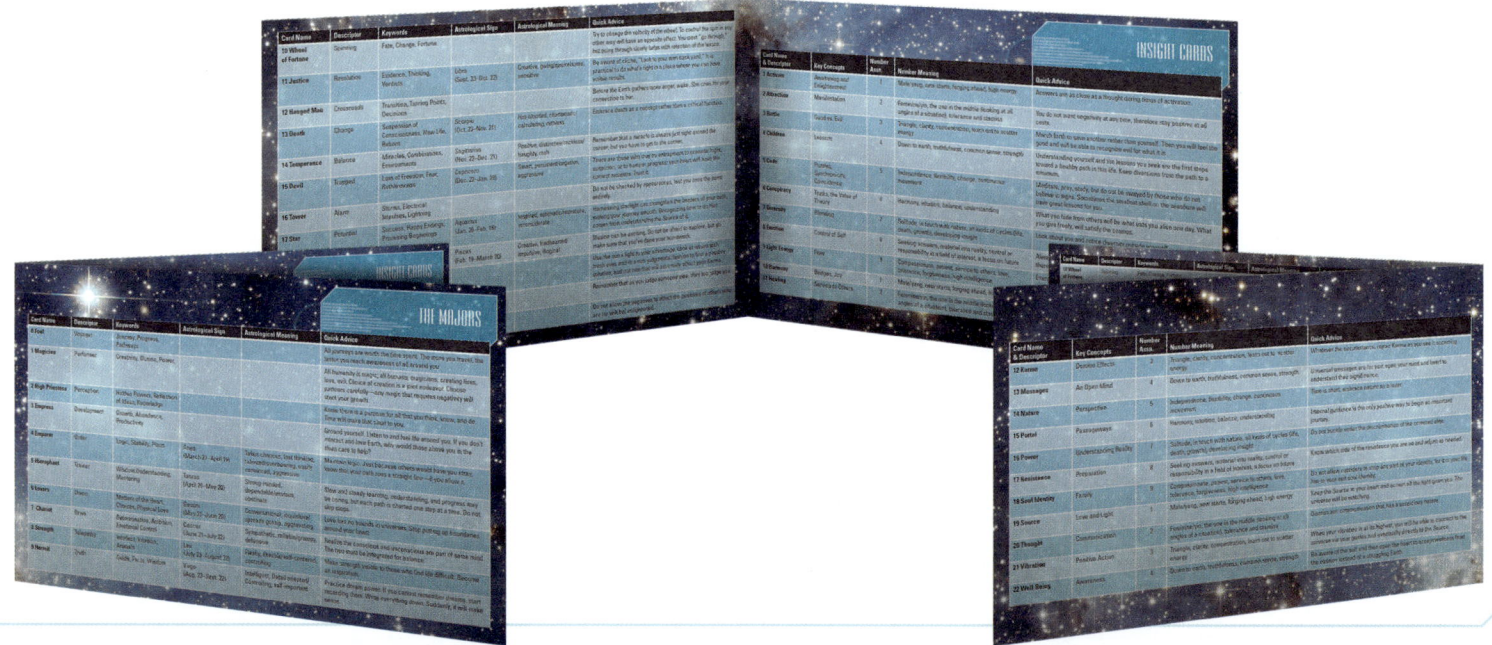

PART II.

THE MAJORS

The Major Arcana in the Tarot deck are the big guns. These twenty-two cards work with important issues within your life and give you concrete ideas for moving forward or solving the big-picture problems. Every card has an important message to bring to you—there are no minor explanations. The Majors instruct you to: Listen! Think! Act!

Here you will find both upright and reversed meanings, directing you to the specifics of your life. The Advice provided works much as the insights given on the Insight cards: *Move along slowly or quickly, but move along*. Think about these things, listen to your heart. Then put a plan together. The advice offered gives an overview of what the whole card should mean to you.

You will find astrological references on twelve of the Majors that reflect personalities or concepts that should be considered.

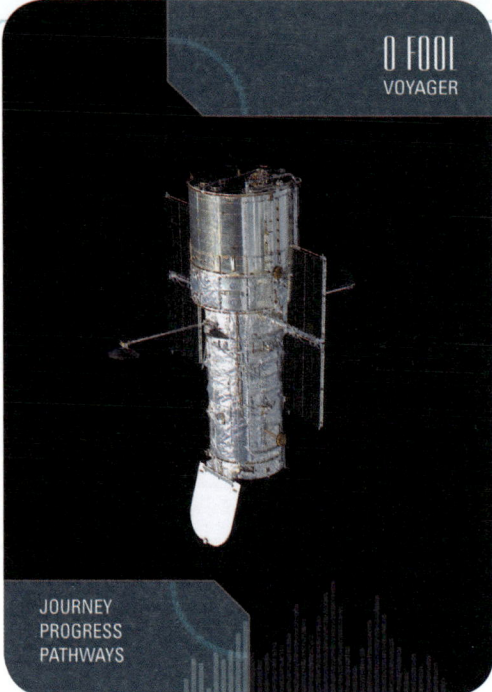

Keyword: Journey, Progress, Pathways

Upright: The Fool, beginning the journey of life as a child of the universe, moves through life sometimes thinking…and sometimes just playing. Are you ready to make a commitment voyage toward your own enlightenment? Now is the time to begin this new path, aware that you will have a journey unlike those taken before.

Reversed: You seem to be stumbling along your path. This is not necessarily a bad thing, but it will require some effort to understand what options are likely to move you forward and what will keep you unsteady and slow. Open your eyes. It's time to readjust your thinking.

Advice: The Fool is but a visitor to the skies—a traveler. Making his or her way across the cosmos, the lessons are learned one by one, taught by experience and listening to the whispers of space. Of course, in the universe, beyond Earthly knowledge, there is no sound, so the traveler must consider inspiration that comes from within connected to those who are without. The beings watching the voyager's progress gently (most times) nudge this fearless human to awakening and enlightenment, but the path is not always clear or smooth. This is how it is meant to be.

> All journeys are worth the time spent. The more you travel at this time, the faster you will reach open awareness of all that is around you.

0 FOOL
VOYAGER

Keywords: Creativity, Illusion, Power

Upright: All the world is a stage in the eyes of some and certainly the Magician can forward the illusion of many things with the tools at hand. What are your tools for moving forward in your lessons of life? Self-confidence runs high now and because of this, your creativity and the power it brings will allow you to flourish. When this card appears, know that if there are unclear things (illusions) around you; this is the time to recognize them for what they are and use them to your advantage.

Reversed: Do not let the sneaky inner voices of a lack of self-confidence destroy your hard work. If you don't act, it could. Though your tools of the trade (including your intellect and your speaking ability) may seem rusty, you'd better pull the curtain closed around you and pretend you are confident like the great wizard you are. (That, you know, leads to the real thing.)

Advice: Illusions and reality are the same on Earth. It is only the individual who chooses to separate them. Once you make up your mind to understand both your tools and the path you are on, the illusions will turn into visible reality. Be careful to stay alert to the possibility that your reality could become illusion if you do not remain confident and maintain your willpower.

All of humanity is magic and all humans are magicians: creating lives, creating love, creating evil. The choice of creation is a joint endeavor. Choose your partners carefully because any magic that requires negativity to survive will stunt your personal growth.

2 HIGH PRIESTESS — PERCEPTION

Keywords: Hidden Powers, Reflection of Ideas, Knowledge

Upright: Great knowledge and ancient wisdom are the qualities of the High Priestess. Though she has hidden powers, once they are brought to the surface, they show as strong and true. She has a knowing about herself and the world about her that began with the developing of the Magician's ideas, and has since turned to the reflection of those ideas outward into the universe—a powerful ally is she. What are you reflecting of yourself to the outer world? Do people find comfort in you and come to you for good advice? When they do, try not to push them away, for your role with this card is to assist all journeyers to their next stop with uplifting comfort and love. The High Priestess has plenty to go around. Remember that when someone learns from you, it is most important that you learn from him/her.

Reversed: When the card of the High Priestess is reversed, there is deception in the mix. It could be you deceiving yourself or a deceit by someone else. There is also the possibility that someone on the outskirts of your being could be intentionally cruel and uncooperative. Dig deep for that "knowing" you are recognized for, so that identifications can be made.

Advice: Those in the heavens know so much more because they are viewing circumstances from a higher elevation. If you were in a cornfield, standing on the ground, you would not be able to see very much. But if you had a step ladder and you climbed above the stalks, the area would be much clearer to you. The beings outside Earth's form are much further up and therefore can see all that you cannot. This is why you should listen to what knowledge they send to your heart. Your unconscious mind knows the right answer to your questions because of this communication technique. Hone the skill.

If there is one thing that the High Priestess concept gives forth for humanity, it is to know with all your heart that there is a purpose for all that you think, know, and do. Time will make that clear to you.

Keywords: Growth, Abundance, Productivity

Upright: The Empress is deeply in touch with all things natural on and above the earth, including the Earth itself. She monitors growth and is highly aware of all life cycles. If you've received this card, then the notion of getting back to the beginning of things is an important one. Think of a flower: planted, watered, grown. This thinking applies to ideas, personal growth, and childbirth. You can see to the heart of a matter and then project that outward to assist those needing clarity regarding a family matter. This could be your family or another's.

Reversed: This is a case of exact opposite. Things are not productive. There is little, if any, growth. If you are looking to have children, there may be fertility difficulties.

Advice: Every home in the universe, whether solid ground, gaseous cloud, toxic air, or any other variation, has the distinct life force that gives life and a home to the beings inhabiting it. Once inhabitants begin to overly abuse the home, its power, its health, and its own emotional well being, things begin to disintegrate. Then the home becomes not a home, but a prison. This Empress and her following work upon the Earth's waters. Whether you consider your home the Earth as a whole, or a house sitting upon it, nurture the place you live so that you will continue to have shelter.

Ground yourself in all you do. Listen to and feel the life that is around you—not just other humans—but those other individuals who do not often hear your praise: animals, plants, the Earth herself. If you don't interact and love your home Earth, why would those above you in the skies care to help you through tribulations?

Keywords: Logic, Stability, Plans

Astrological Sign: Aries (March 21–April 19)

Aries traits: takes chances, fast thinking, talented/overbearing, easily convinced, aggressive

Upright: The Emperor is one who knows the law and takes great comfort in the idea that to follow a plan as you journey takes you more quickly to your goal. Keep your eyes on the prize is his motto. There is a set way of doing things that will guarantee success. Don't stray from your ideals, your beliefs, or plans—unless they can be logically discarded for better circumstances.

Reversed: If reversed, there is rebellion in the mix, as well as illogical thinking. You may see the path needed, but you are drawn away from it to follow a whim. Beware the road you take. It could lead to more poor choices.

Advice: The Star Being taking the role of Emperor in this card has your best interests at heart. He knows all the roads to success and asks merely that you listen to his advice, for it is sound and will accommodate outcomes that can only enhance your passage to enlightenment.

Maintain your logic at all costs. Just because others would have you stray from critical thinking, feel safe in knowing that your path to the stars runs along a straight line—if you allow it.

Keywords: Wisdom, Understanding, Mentoring

Astrological Sign: Taurus (April 20–May 20)

Taurus traits: strong-minded, dependable/envious, obstinate

Upright: You may find that a personal teacher or institution has something important to impart to you. Lessons are at hand, and though they may seem tedious and monotonous, the value can not be overstated. You must experience the mundane to recognize the spectacular. Are your beliefs solid? Have you understood the nature of your issue and identified the secrets that have accompanied it up until now? If so, you are ready to take good advice from a knowledgeable and ageless individual and to move forward.

Reversed: There may be an unreasonable aspect to the advice someone is giving you. Ideas seem old, out of place, or lacking luster. Is this all there is?

Advice: The Hierophant is a mentor and teacher acting on the behalf of a full group of galactic races. This is a massive undertaking outlined into meticulous steps that will bring mankind to an understanding of its place in the universe. When this card turns up, it is a reminder that there is much to be learned and that it can not be taken in all at once. These teachings include spiritual destinies, knowledge of the ages, and determinations of culpability for decisions and lives lived. This card indicates that one will be able to move on once experience is gained.

Slow and steady learning, understanding, and progress may be boring, but each path is charted one step at a time. Each step has its importance. Do not skip steps.

6 LOVERS — UNION

MATTERS OF THE HEART
CHOICES
PHYSICAL LOVE

Keywords: Matters of the Heart, Choices, Physical Love

Astrological Sign: Gemini (May 21–June 20)

Gemini traits: conversational, inquisitive/spreads gossip, aggravating

Upright: The Lovers card brings romance into your life, and though it usually signifies a physical love, here we find that there is love that covers a much wider concept. Love is all around you right now in everything you do, everything you feel, everything you think. If this is not the case, it's time for you to make that happen. Those around you see you in a very positive light and you'll want to maintain it by being responsive to their needs. Care for those about you as they care for you—and they do care, even if they hide it from you.

Reversed: You may feel lonely at this time, for you fear that things have not developed in the manner you'd hoped. This is not entirely true because you are not accurately seeing the real picture. Your "down" attitude has placed you in an atmosphere where you feel thwarted and physically separated from the things and people who really matter to you. Wake up.

Advice: The Lovers card symbolizes the love that comes to all humanity from the stars. Are there those in the universe who do not feel this way? Yes, but they are insignificant in the scheme of things. Step outside your enclosures and open your heart to receive what is available to you: love, greater intelligence, connections, and wonder.

Love has no bounds within universes. Stop putting up boundaries around your heart.

Keywords: Determination, Ambition, Emotional Control

Astrological Sign: Cancer (June 21–July 22)

Cancer traits: sympathetic, reliable/grumpy, defensive

Upright: The Chariot is the drive and determination behind one's ambition, and riding the skies with specific focus toward goals is indicated here. The mode of movement is not as important as your will to get where you need to be. Be in control of your emotions now. Identify your plan and then drive your conscious mind forward to success.

Reversed: A voyage that you are excited to take could be delayed if you don't control your desires, or you could become more about material gain than enlightenment.

Advice: The vehicles of the skies would seem to be some strange and varied craft, but this is only a small part of the larger picture. The mode of transportation is really your body, linking you to the foundation of the Earth, but well aware that the universe awaits and you need only connect your mind and spirit with your body to travel to it.

Realize that your conscious and unconscious are all part of the same mind. To serve your journey in any meaningful way, the two must be integrated for balance. Picture the two parts of your mind moving together and then see the star path burst out in front of you.

Keywords: Intellect, Intuition, Animals

Astrological Sign: Leo (July 23–August 22)

Leo traits: flashy, likeable/self-centered, controlling

Upright: The Strength card brings forth a "knowing" about those around you in the form of intuition or telepathy. You feel strong in the way you are able to communicate and to understand easily what those around you are trying to relay. It's almost as though you have lived this time before, because the answers to your questions seem to have been well thought out and prepared before you've ever asked. This card also brings forth an intense understanding and love for animals of all natures—including those that have repulsed you in the past. An even more interesting development here is that animals seem to know your thoughts as well. You also may have the feeling that someone has something important to share with you—at least from their eyes. Listen.

Reversed: The messages you are receiving are not clear. You are hearing someone or understanding someone, but it feels wrong. Could something be missing? Keep your heart open so that you don't miss the true significance.

Advice: Beings from other universes and dimensions do not have physical love connections to humans; however, they do have very strong love ties that are fed to them through the Source and then on to our hearts. Love may or may not be a concept for some, but no matter, because the connection to us is the same. Keep the heart and mind open and consider that you may not know all, but you can accept all connections of a positive vein into the heart.

Make your strength visible to those who find life difficult. Become an inspiration to them, for it is they who will be your teachers one day.

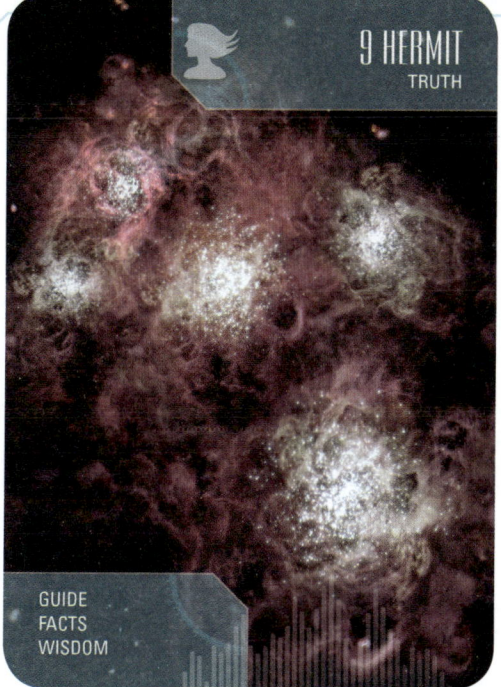

Keywords: Guide, Facts, Wisdom

Astrological Sign: Virgo (August 23–September 22)

Virgo traits: intelligent, detail oriented/controlling, self-important

Upright: Someone who you may not have noticed before will be available to guide you toward your goals. Wisdom from this source has been gained through experience and trials, so you can depend upon it to help you reach your outcome in a positive fashion. There is also someone far away who is associated with this card, an individual or group that has journeyed much over the years. You, too, may be offered a trip. Keep your "light" handy.

Reversed: You may become stranded—in your mind, your quest, or your physical travels. Delays or plans change (for the worst). Stay on your toes.

Advice: Know that in the universe there are many wise guides who help individuals and groups to understand the wisdom of their true beginnings. Look inward to understand such invitations to gain knowledge. Sometimes information and plans are "downloaded" while you sleep or dream. Be cognizant of dreams that are very real in context, because they may not be dreams at all, but experiences. If you'd like a visit in your dreams, ask for one in meditation. Be sure to ask to remember it and that it be of a positive nature from a loving star being. "Keep the light on."

Concentrate and practice your dream power. It is more important than ever that the universe be able to communicate with you in this fashion. If you cannot remember your dreams, practice appropriate dream recording. Write everything down. Suddenly, it will make sense.

Keywords: Fate, Change, Fortune

Upright: The wheel is always spinning. Where your situation fits onto the wheel at this current time will give you an indication of how to view it. Are you on the upswing? If yes, you will be able to see now—or very soon—positive aspects arriving in your life. If on the down side of the wheel, things will begin to look up eventually. Always be prepared for the next spin.

Reversed: Still spinning; a reverse speaks of a delay in positive phases, a negative stop (or one coming). Just remember, the wheel never stays still, so this, too, shall pass.

Advice: The spinning of any mobile craft can be seen in the wheel and this spin offers a view of all sides of an issue from above and on the Earth. It matters not where the wheel slows or speeds up. All places allow the individual to learn right from wrong where the wheel stops. Those in the universe learn as much from our individual spin as we may learn from theirs.

Try to change the velocity of the wheel. To control the spin in any other way will have an opposite effect. You must "go through," but going through slowly helps with the retention of the lesson and may keep you from having to "relearn" it.

10 WHEEL OF FORTUNE
SPINNING

Keywords: Evidence, Thinking, Verdicts

Astrological Sign: Libra (September 23–October 22)

Libra traits: creative, giving/quarrelsome, sensitive

Upright: This card predicts that there is an individual or group who is being analytical in their thinking as they research facts to build a case. Laws are tested. There is a time of trial and error, but the verdict will clearly send someone in the right direction or along the right path. Make sure you understand the issues and have the correct facts, so that any verdict brought down will be a fair one.

Reversed: The answers are not clear and the research is incomplete. Things could be postponed or entirely reversed unless you are very careful. Do your homework.

Advice: There's no doubt that many outerworld organizations and individuals are collecting facts, considering evidence, and preparing a verdict about mankind. You are being watched to see if you can interact in love with those in other habitats. It is recognized that this is not an "all or nothing" scenario, for there are those who serve others and those who serve self. Make sure you are one of the former.

Be aware of your cliché that says, "Look to your own back yard." When it comes to justifications for and against any situation or emotion, it is only practical to do what's right in a place where you can have visible results.

Keywords: Transition, Turning Points, Decisions

Upright: The Hanged Man seems to be left with little alternative, but that's not quite true. Though he is upside-down in a tree (traditionally in the Rider-Waite images), there is still room for the right decisions to be made that will bring him down to Earth. Transform yourself at a crossroads into someone who can think clearly, note what has gone wrong in the past, and learn how to prepare in order to keep yourself upright and in the game. Since your answers will come from within, this is the time to meditate seriously.

Reverse: You (or someone) passes the tests and flings ridicule or ways of self-punishment away. Keep a steady stance and stand away from the tree!

Advice: When one is on one's head, whether in a tree or in any manner of state, the individual is not connected to the Earth. Though it is the goal to have connections to the skies and to the Earth, at this crossroads, it's important to stay grounded and connected to your planet. The universe welcomes you outwards, but before you can go out, you must be connected to something within—that would be your home and your heart.

Before the Earth gathers more anger, wake. She cries for your connection to her.

12 HANGED MAN
CROSSROADS

Keywords: Suspension of Consciousness, New Life, Reborn

Astrological Sign: Scorpio (October 23–November 21)

Scorpio traits: hot-blooded, charismatic/calculating, ruthless

Upright: Though the Death card does not usually mean death, here there is a death to self in order to visualize change. It is not a physical death—unless other cards support it—but rather a suspension of consciousness in order to connect to the Source. This best happens through meditation where you will be given the information you need to rearrange your physical life.

Reversed: The change will be difficult. The path to meditation and Source will be littered with obstacles. Take the high road by realizing that you must run the obstacle course with confidence to get through it.

Advice: In the stars, death is less a word of endings and more a word of connections to all around the cosmos. All beings outside the Earth move in and out of change—death—routinely and without fear. With every new connection to Spirit, there is a death to the old ways.

Embrace death as a concept rather than a critical function.

Keywords: Miracles, Combinations, Environments

Astrological Sign: Sagittarius (November 22–December 21)

Sagittarius traits: positive, distinctive/reckless, haughty, rash

Upright: You have a way with combining things and ideas that spur incredible creativity, but make sure there is a balance in all you do. Tipping one way or another makes magical formulas work differently—or not at all. There is someone indicated here who is good at working with many things that might not normally be put together. On the Earth, this person may have ideas to transform the negativity in the environment for the better. Miracles happen around the Temperance card.

Reversed: The magic formula is "off" and does not produce reliable outcomes. Time to clean up the mess.

Advice: Maintaining a balance has not always been an easy task for outworlders. This happens because the number of variables that are evident during any kind of contact are far reaching, bringing varied outcomes—some good, some not. If you interact with the universe, remain as balanced as possible, so that you do not upset your life by adding the universe's magic to yours before you are ready for it.

Remember that a miracle is always just right around the corner, but you have to get to the corner first.

Keywords: Loss of Freedom, Fear, Ruthlessness

Astrological Sign: Capricorn (December 22–January 19)

Capricorn traits: smart, persistent/negative, aggressive

Upright: An individual finding this card in a reading should be on the lookout for entrapment issues. This could involve any part of life, but be assured that someone has gotten (or will get) the better of you. Options seem limited. You've lost your self-confidence. You feel demoralized and can't see a way out of your problems. Try not to panic.

Reversed: You may have hit on an idea just in the nick of time to save you from losing your freedom. There is a fine line, however, and it could be easy to slip back into the muck.

Advice: Governments around the Earth have had much to hide over the years and it appears that it could be some time (if ever) before every issue comes to light. This is widespread throughout Earth's continents. There is the act of presenting fear of Star Beings (in the form of entertainment and ridicule) to Earth's personage. It's best to ignore the negativity and interact with the universe directly via your own mind/body/spirit methods. Keep protections up via your Source to keep out intruders you do not wish to invade your mind.

Your government officials (and others you may not be aware of) may try entrapment methods to promote fright, suspicion, or to hamper your progress to enlightenment, but your heart will have the correct answers. Trust it.

16 TOWER — ALARM

Keywords: Storms, Electrical Impulses, Lightning

Upright: The Tower card gives a strong warning of destruction of teachings brought forth under false pretenses—and not in a calming way. There are lightning strikes, storms, and great battles around this card. It could involve someone dealing with electrical mechanisms or computers, but again, in a negative way. Physical storms are possible or a shock that affects you deeply. Someone could be having a mental lapse of judgment that is hurtful. Water may be involved: storms, showers . . . . Take cover as soon as possible, because whatever the storm entails (emotional or physical), it's not to be ignored.

Reversed: More shock, possibly by something you've witnessed. Acts of the Source rain down on you. Your current cover has holes in it. Get out the tarp!

Advice: The towers of nuclear possibilities must be closely monitored by the outerworld, least someone sound the alarm to fire. There is the possibility that these things may need to be put into non-working order to save your planet. Those from the stars wonder at your carelessness.

Do not be shocked by appearances, lest you miss the point entirely.

Keywords: Success, Happy Endings, Promising Beginnings

Astrological Sign: Aquarius (January 20–February 18)

Aquarius traits: inspired, optimistic/immature, inconsiderate

Upright: The Star is a beautiful card to pull from the deck because it allows wondrous starlight to fall down to you from the Heavens. Your hopes, your dreams, and your reality have a bright future, and you can feel the light of love in your heart. Right now, people see you as a rising star, a successful individual who can withstand anything. And they are certainly right!

Reversed: Though starlight is strong and filled with energy, it does not do well to use it unwisely. You might experience burnout and then your feelings of "high" may fall.

Advice: Starlight and the stars themselves are for everyone—human or otherwise. The energy that is offered is the fuel that we all use to move forward through our days. It is not endless, however, and learning to balance the glow is imperative.

Harnessing starlight can strengthen the borders of your path, making your journey smooth. Recognizing how to do that comes from understanding the Source of it.

18 MOON PHASES

Keyword: Mystery, Instinct, Discovery

Astrological Sign: Pisces (February 19–March 20)

Pisces traits: creative, kindhearted/impulsive, illogical

Upright: The phases of Earth's moon have more to do with humans following their instincts than anything else. There are often illusions and deceptions beneath the moon, just outside the light, that can affect involuntary desires. This is a good time to bring those desires into the light, so that they can be examined and acted upon (or not). Many have psychic abilities and now is the time to use them to make changes that can move one to a smoother path. Look into your heart for answers.

Reversed: Any deceptions now can be discovered and changed as need be, but you do feel "off" for some reason that you cannot see.

Advice: The light of the moon is not as bright as the starlight in many cases, and this means that energies are not quite as strong, or they may even be invisible. The idea is to stay inside the light and push away darkness at all costs.

Illusion can be exciting sometimes. Do not be afraid to explore, but do make sure that you know the way back.

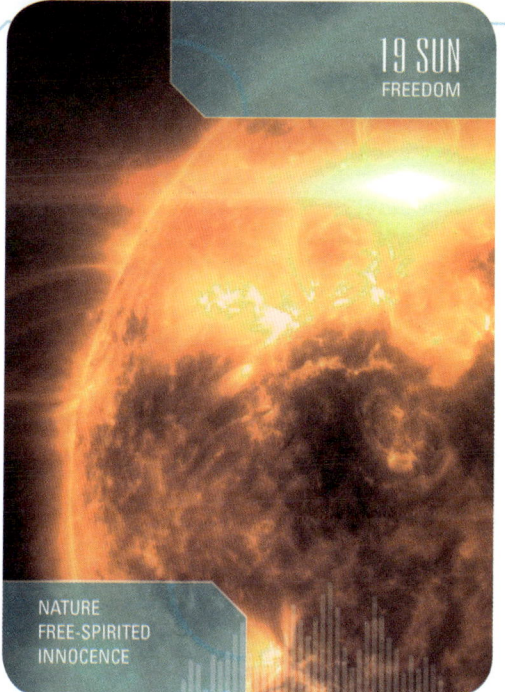

19 SUN — INDEPENDENCE

Keywords: Nature, Free-Spirited, Innocence

Upright: When the sun is shining, all is right with the Earth. This would be the same for anyone drawing this card. A happy time and high momentum for projects can be felt. Especially warranted are plants or any nature endeavors that may interest you. Test your wings and feel your independence. This card lightens any messages around it. Much opportunity flows now. Children are also highlighted.

Reversed: Calm down just a bit; you may be overdoing the joy. That can get in the way of your seeing the reality of a situation.

Advice: The Sun is a very important star for the universe as a whole. Were it not for its true being, varied life forms could not exist. Yet the heat can be destructive under the right conditions. The Sun does send away the shadows that oftentimes can screen reality. So if you feel as though you need to understand the universe, do it with the full light of the Sun. There is the opportunity of true recognition now.

> *Use the sun's light to your advantage, for it will not be long until the moon approaches with its illusion. Look at issues with fresh eyes and in a non-judgmental fashion. In this way, you will find a positive solution, and not one that will adversely affect your Karma.*

Keyword: Decisions, Outlook, Finality

Upright: You've done all the work and collected all the research. Now is the time to consider that important critical decision, then make it. The heart is as involved as the mind, so allow prayers to move you toward the right decision—especially if this is a situation of life and death. Don't feel like your life is coming to a close just because your fate seems to be staring you in the eyes. This is just the beginning of your enlightenment.

Reversed: Keep an open mind and fight that part of you that wants to close off the rest of the world. If you find yourself turning away from decisions that must be made, return before it's too late.

Advice: It is now time to awaken to the world around you—it is much bigger than you ever imagined and your part in it is sealed. You just have to open your mind to the value that you bring to the universe. You must integrate into the races outside humanity and accept the responsibilities that will come with it.

> *Remember that as you judge someone else, they too judge you. How will you look in their eyes?*

20 JUDGMENT
RESULTS

Keywords: Rebirth, Reincarnation, Celebration

Upright: If you draw this card, know that a time of celebration is upon you, for you have achieved the right to go through a spiritual rebirth. Reincarnation is also indicated because to reach this point, you've had to live many lives and learn many lessons. This new emotional growth will provide you with a fresh start and exciting possibilities. Who will you invite to share your gala?

Reversed: You may be leaving the party. If you do, this means that lessons thought learned have to be gone through yet again. Do you see your fresh start elsewhere? If you do, turn around—it's the wrong start.

Advice: Rebirth into a universal community is cause for celebration, but also a time for reflection. How have you gotten this far? Have you hurt anyone along the way? A new destiny means cleaning up the debris from the old one before putting on the new suit of life. It won't take you long, but forgetting those who helped you along the path puts a Karmic debt on your shoulders.

> Do not allow the negatives of those in your world to affect the positives of others who are (or will be) enlightened.

21 WORLD
RENEWAL

Insight Cards

Information provided for the insight cards comes from the universe and is given as matters and materials to think about as you live your daily life. While the Tarot gives you specifics—positive and negative—the insight cards gently massage your situation into a comfortable plan that you can immediately put into place for the good. The number associations provide a backbone or basis to your situation, along with any emotional practicalities that need to be considered at the moment. These numbers can be used singularly along with the card or combined to give a full concept to discover for the whole reading (by reducing the final number count to a single digit).

Key Concept: Awakening and Enlightenment
Number Association: 1

1. Male/yang, new starts, forging ahead, high energy

Advice: Though to activate does involve the balancing of Chakras, there is more to be done. First, take the time to put an action plan together that works with the Higher Self in a way that awakens you to the reality of beings from other universes. Then the Chakra work will smoothly improve all your encounters. Your blood is filled with the DNA that allows creation. Activation is a full-body affair that requires you to release all negativities and see the world you live on for what it is: a living entity in its own right. With that knowledge, ground yourself to Earth and reach up to the stars with your mind.

Answers are as close as a thought during times of activation.

Key Concept: Manifestation
Number Association: 2

2. Feminine/yin, the one in the middle (looking at all angles of a situation), tolerance and stamina

Advice: Not all that you want to attract is good for you. Therefore, when your heart's desire does not come, do not become frustrated or sad. Something better is there for you. Attracting this new positive "thing" should be a top priority. Know that each thought you have is projected outward into the universe for eventual manifestation. Attraction of such thoughts comes in varied forms and in varied lifetimes. The stronger the thought, the more likely that your attraction will take place. This is significant because if your thoughts root in the negative, that is what you will draw to you. These things do not take place instantly in most humans' lives, but rather slowly over a lifetime or longer—when you least expect it in many cases.

You do not want negativity to slap you in the face at any time, therefore stay positive at all costs.

Key Concept: Good vs. Evil
Number Association: 3

3. Triangle, clarity, concentration, learn not to scatter energy

Advice: Whether in battles of the heart or physical battles in the world, always ask: why? If you don't have a good reason, should you not abandon your position? Is your battle larger than yourself? You can not change another, so reel in your prejudice. Do not allow negativity to gain hold over your mind in any way, for this is when you lose the battle.

March forth with the desire to save another rather than yourself. Then you will feel the good and will be able to recognize evil for what it is and laugh in the face of those who would in other times terrify you.

3 BATTLE

Key Concept: Lessons
Number Association: 4

4. Down to earth, truthfulness, common sense, strength

Advice: It would be good to understand that we are all children in the scheme of things, and each individual is standing along the path for return to the Source. Therefore, if you feel superior in any way, step back. Make room for others on the path to understand what you think you have gleaned from your lessons. You may find that your journey is more closely aligned to your counterparts' than you initially thought. The children of the stars are always clamoring to work with humanity, for outerworld youngsters have already mastered the lessons that you are striving to master at this time. The children from the stars are patient and wait for you to compile all your research and beliefs about them. You still have to "climb the mountain" and go deep into your own psyche to really understand what purpose you hold in the experience, but there is time.

> *Understanding yourself and the lessons you seek are the first steps toward a healthy path in this life—and in past or future lives as well. Keep diversions from the path to a minimum.*

4 CHILDREN

Key Concept: Puzzles, Synchronicity, Coincidence
Number Association: 5

5. Independence, flexibility, change, continuous movement

Advice: There are codes all around you every day. The challenge is to recognize your connection to them. The Earth has turned into one giant puzzle at this time in its being. Mother Earth wants and needs to be understood, but she speaks in code, in synchronicity, in mystery. Solving the code is imperative. Finding out what signs are given specifically to you—whether from the Earth, the Source, or via your awakening process—has never been more important to your survival and joy. Take note of strange coincidences in your life—they often are herding you down a coded path where you need to be. Ignore them and things can become difficult. Study the signs that you do not understand. Discuss them with like-minded individuals.

Meditate, pray, study, but do not be swayed by those who do not believe in signs. Sometimes the smallest shell on the seashore will have great lessons for you.

5 CODE

Key Concept: Truths, the Value of Theory
Number Association: 6

6. Harmony, intuition, balance, understanding

Advice: It is difficult sometimes not to fall into believing conspiracy theories when you are looking at all the facts and conjecture that go so smoothly in one specific direction. It is doubly problematic when those around you try to hide truths from you. There is no need to bother with conspiracy—everything will come out in the wash, as humans sometimes say. And if payment is required, this is handled by the Source and you need not make it a worry. Worry lowers vibration. Beware conspiracies that drag you into a pit of negativity and a lack of understanding. Embrace those who will serve the world on a grand basis. Make sure you understand which is which.

What you hide from others will be what eats you alive one day. What you give freely, will satisfy the cosmos.

Key Concept: Blending
Number Association: 7

7. Solitude, in touch with nature, all kinds of cycles (life, death, growth), developing insight

Advice: If there were one lesson that rose to the top for the Earth, it would be that of diversity, for this has not been accomplished in any time of the planet's existence. Just remember, until the people of Earth recognize that each individual is also a part of another, and another—all the way to the Source—the universe will never be one with you, and you will never be one with anyone else. The sooner you become comfortable with diversity among races and species the better. Embrace diversity in beings, experiences, vision, and decisions. Respect every part of your world. Then look outward with the joy of knowing that it is even more diverse in the skies than within your own life. Being diverse allows one to experience many realities, many lives, many beings. Those in the universe demand diversity because the lessons accompanying such are the quickest way to be noticed by the Source.

Look about you and notice diversity outside yourself.

7 DIVERSITY

Key Concept: Control of Self
Number Association: 8

8. Seeking answers, material into reality, control or responsibility in a field of interest, a focus on future

Advice: Though emotion is not always understood from moment to moment, it has the capacity to heal or hurt. Therefore, understanding how your emotions affect your world and the stars will deaden conflict and promote connection. Stay positive; it raises your vibration and keeps your body healthy. Controlling emotions in a happy way keeps negativity from being drawn to you. Like attracts like. The cliché that "opposites attract" does not bode well when discussing emotional conflict. The key is to identify the emotion, understand why you are feeling it, and then do everything you can to maintain a happy outlook.

Always look for the silver lining. Whether you believe it or not, it's there.

Key Concept: Flow
Number Association: 9

9. Compassionate, patient, service to others, love, tolerance, forgiveness, high intelligence

Advice: Light and energy connect every being and every thing to the Source. Remaining positive allows the Source to flow more and more energy back to you to provide healing, joy, and high vibration within your life. The higher the vibration, the more energy is available to you for the manifestation of both life experience and the happiness that everyone strives for. It is a massive continuing circle. Never allow energy to fall or wan lest the circle be broken and negativity weaken you. You should expect conflict from time to time, but try not to be part of it. It is in your best interest to maintain the highest path of energy so that the universe can connect with you in good time within that circle. Conserve your internal light for growth. Then create more light energy with your enthusiasm of things in your daily life, sending that out to all who will accept it.

Energy shared is love spread.

9 ENERGY

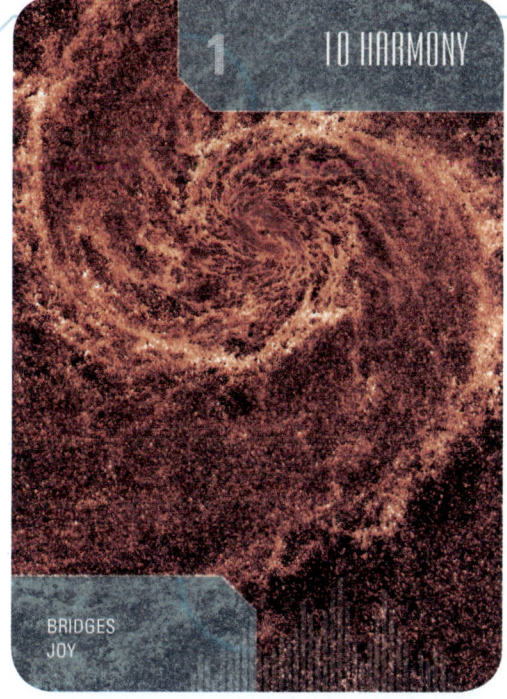

Key Concept: Bridges, Joy
Number Association: 1 (reduced from 1+0=1)

1. Male/yang, new starts, forging ahead, high energy

Advice: Creating harmony is done at the soul level, so you only have yourself to blame if things go wrong. It is time to repair or build bridges among you and also to the stars. Identify the links that promote relaxation, joy, and love, and then breathe them into your being. Reach out to your Higher Self, your guides, and other star beings for assistance in maintaining traits that support unity. In the quiet moments of a harmonious life, you will be able to touch the stars and interact with those around you in a way that allows growth for both parties. Discord has no value. Consider that everything around you and every being you meet wishes to live in harmony, and that you are the one who keeps that accord alive by merely bearing witness to your own growth.

Harmony is the first step to love.

10 HARMONY

Key Concept: Service to Others
Number Association: 2 (reduced from 1+1=2)

2. Feminine/yin, the one in the middle (looking at all angles of a situation), tolerance and stamina.

Advice: Healing both the conscious and the unconscious mind is imperative if you are to move forward. Clear the Chakras, balance them, and then meditate for the answers to the obstacles in your life. Healing, too, can involve a service to others that can be imperative to your life pattern. Learning to heal in a variety of ways then becomes a fruitful way to raise your own vibration. Is there someone near you who is unwell in the body, the mind, or the spirit? It would benefit the both of you to connect and share wellness and healing. Sometimes this is as simple as accepting a person for who he or she is without being judgmental. Other times, prayers for the healing of disease done as a group make all the difference.

Identify what healing is needed and by who. Then proceed accordingly.

11 HEALING

Key Concept: Domino Effects
Number Association: 3 (reduced from 1+2=3)

3. Triangle, clarity, concentration, learn not to scatter energy

Advice: Manage your Karma by not forgetting your lessons. Develop your own "right" beliefs and theories so that you do not damage your future selves. Understand that any lesson not learned is a lesson to be repeated (as often as needed). Forever is a long time. This may be time to look at past or future lives within meditation or hypnosis, for it can only help to know what lessons were not learned in those lives that will be repeating in your current one. Having a plan of correction for bad Karma can ease your journey. Good Karma, of course, usually passes without even a thought, for it requires no amendment or adjustment. Even so, make good Karma at every opportunity for it will assist you in all your lives—especially the one you are currently in.

Whatever the circumstance, repair Karma as you see it occurring.

13 MESSAGES

Key Concept: An Open Mind
Number Association: 4 (reduced from 1+3=4)

4. Down to earth, truthfulness, common sense, strength

Advice: Bodies, people, animals, plants, the universe, and the Source all send messages. Some are good, some not; but not listening promotes missing things that matter. Push away the human desire to be self-absorbed and open your heart to *hear* your path. Messages will be many and diverse as time moves forward—weather, Earth, space, internal, senses—all will be affected. It will be your choice whether to heed the communications offered or to let it go like yesterday's news. Our advice is not to turn a blind eye to the things that are manifested in front of you. If you do not understand what you are seeing, research, identify, discuss. The time for you to remember who you are is now, so noticing the messages about you becomes imperative. Look more closely. There's always more. Become aware.

Universal messages are for you; you only need open your mind and heart to understand their significance to your life.

Key Concept: Perspective
Number Association: 5 (reduced from 1+4=5)

5. Independence, flexibility, change, continuous movement

Advice: Nature is a vast life form that works in collaboration with the Mother Earth and the universal skies. Each life being looks at the world from a different viewpoint. Enabling yourself to see the world from outside yourself will give strength to the natural world. This allows you to walk a smooth passage. Nature is part of your life cycle and requires respect—or you may find that it will not respect you. The smallest insect all the way up to the human condition, the Earth will maintain your life and heal your heart if you but listen to her calls. You do not want to make her angry. Even the full universe cannot bring you back from that.

Time is short; embrace nature as a lover.

14 NATURE

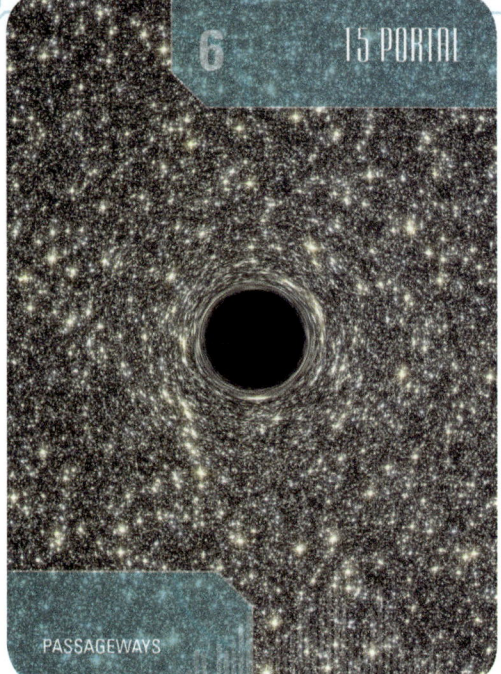

Key Concept: Passageways
Number Association: 6 (reduced from 1+5=6)

6. Harmony, intuition, balance, understanding

Advice: Movement between worlds, times, and relationships can occur in many ways. Connections can be strengthened by understanding that one world is only your illusion. To see more, you must be more. The portal will open when you are ready. Portals require that you identify who is using the pathway and where the path leads. If it is you traveling, know that certain decisions have to be made before any path is taken. Research, understand, and make the best plans possible. Notice that some conduits may be dead ends. Ignore popular opinion when you are considering portals.

Internal guidance is the only positive way to begin an important journey.

15 PORTAL

Key Concept: Understanding Reality
Number Association: 7 (reduced from 1+6=7)

7. Solitude, in touch with nature, all kinds of cycles (life, death, growth), developing insight

Advice: Finding your own power in any situation will lead you along the correct passage. You need not be the most powerful, you need only to be aware of your own place in your reality. Power can be a wonderful thing if one knows how to fit it successfully into life. However, oftentimes those you have put into power do not have your highest good in mind, and rather they look out for the self, refusing to share any of the spoils. But fighting the good fight is not as good an idea as you might think, for the strategy thrown back at you will be meant as both a spiritual attack and one that can become physical, leaving you helpless. It is far more important that your power shout out from you in a whisper. When many whisper at one time, the power grows exponentially and you can often win by just sticking together with other like individuals. "Let go and allow the Source" is a good quote to keep in your heart. If enough of you do this, you will have all the power you could ever want.

Do not buckle under the discrimination of the crowned elite.

16 POWER

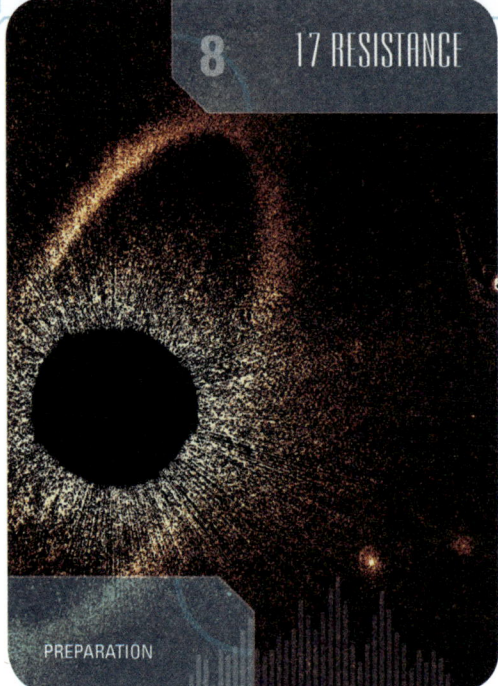

Key Concept: Preparation
Number Association: 8 (reduced from 1+7=8)

8. Seeking answers, material into reality, control or responsibility in a field of interest, a focus on future

Advice: Resisting can be dire, but can also be productive, depending on your circumstances. Find the middle road until you know what is right; then move forward. Refusing to give in to enlightenment or awakening will put you in a state of wrong thinking, thereby lowering your vibration and putting your body at risk. Your brain and DNA are changing even now, preparing you for transformation. It is time to find out exactly what you are resistant to. What are you not allowing into your life that could put you into the labyrinth of learning? Do not hide your heart or refuse to recognize that you are a part of the plan. If, however, you are resisting the negativity of others and making every effort to turn pessimism into love, this is the right path.

Just know which side of the resistance you are on and adjust as needed.

18 SOUL IDENTITY

Key Concept: Family
Number Association: 9 (reduced from 1+8=9)

9. Compassionate, patient, service to others, love, tolerance, forgiveness, high intelligence

Advice: Your soul's identity changes from life to life and minute to minute as it blazes through lessons. The Higher Self has the perfect place of observation and direction, combining the information learned within the family and offering assignments that bring forth a stronger tie to its separate selves. Look to those within your immediate circle for assistance when needed. They may well be family to your Higher Self and part of the lessons you are learning. Know that your family of souls is also in a learning mode and that differences between each of you are only an illusion for a specific set time frame. At some point, the family of souls returns to the Source and travels as one unit.

> *Do not allow outsiders to strip any part of your identity, for it is your lifeline to your unit soul identity.*

Key Concept: Love and Light
Number Association: 1 (reduced from 1+9=10; 1+0=1)

1. Male/yang, new starts, forging ahead, high energy

Advice: This is the "God" or "Source" card and it reminds you that at any given moment, any question of the smallest nature, any assistance that you need, any comfort that is required can send the Source to you with the wings of power and love. Energy spinning, healing light, protective vigor, rest, and transformation can be yours as soon as the thought is released from your mind that you need it. The Source employs any number of supernatural and natural individuals to provide your enlightenment: Archangels, Angels, Guides, even other humans, will show up at the right time to help you with any dilemma you have. Synchronicity is alive. The universe has often been part of this army of goodness and has been there with you at your darkest hours—and your moments of celebration as well.

Keep the Source in your heart and accept all the light that is given you. The universe will be watching for your summons.

19 SOURCE

Key Concept: Communication
Number Association: 2 (reduced from 2+0=2)

2. Feminine/yin, the one in the middle (looking at all angles of a situation), tolerance and stamina

Advice: Use intuitive devices to interact with your Higher Self to send positive messages and thoughts to others. This raises vibration. If you follow thoughtful intuition, listen carefully, because it comes from a higher source. Dismiss all negative thought—this lowers your immune system and can cause illness. Telepathy is also something that will soon be within grasp, as this is the form of communication that is used outside our Earth. When you hear a star being, do not push the thoughts away, for they only want to assist in healing. The brain is capable of great light and can send that energy via thought to those willing to move forward and grow within a community of universal complexities. Do be aware though that not all in the universe will send light. Only listen to positive messages.

Dismiss any communication that has a suspicious nature.

Key Concept: Positive Action
Number Association: 3 (reduced from 2+1=3)

3. Triangle, clarity, concentration, learn to not scatter energy

Advice: There are a multitude of ways to raise vibration: positive thought, loving the self and others, interacting with nature, and good behavior in all you do. Keep your vibrations high in any way you can and at all costs. Your soul's survival depends upon this. There will be a time when only this will allow you to move away from the negativity that is rapidly covering the world.

When your vibration is at its highest, you will be able to connect to the universe via your guides and eventually directly to Source. This is the joy of living.

21 VIBRATION

Key concept: Awareness
Number Association: 4 (reduced from 2+2=4)

4. Down to earth, truthfulness, common sense, strength

Advice: Being well combines the body, mind, and spirit. It stems from the heart outward and invites well energy from the Heavens. If one is aware of the positive state of the self, that person will be able to accept guidance and enlightenment from outside the self and from the stars. The accomplishment is a difficult one because of Earth's societal laws and beliefs—in both science and in organized religion. The universe does not indicate that these beliefs are incorrect, because everyone is entitled to their awareness in their own way. But it is said that well-being does not arrive fully until everything that hinders your lessons is abandoned fully, so that new illumination has room to grow.

Be aware of the self and then open the heart to accept wellness from the cosmos instead of a struggling Earth.

22 WELL BEING

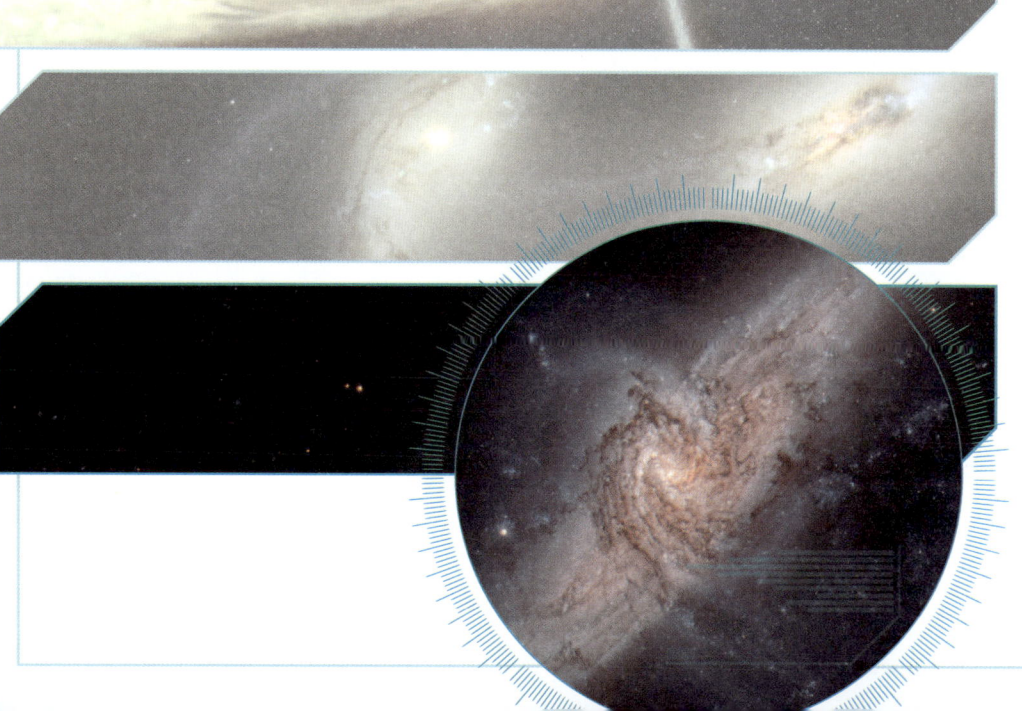

PART III.

CONCLUSION

As you will have noted as you've read over the passages included in this book, the Insight cards' advice is enlightened and shows the desire of the universal beings to see you enlightened, too. This is an indication of high vibration. Once you've begun to use *First Light*, spread your senses outward to the Heavens. Be more aware of the stars and constellations, be cognizant of the satellites and space station (or other things) orbiting our planet Earth. Notice the weather patterns and Earth's communications to us. Become one with all living things—animals, people, plants, other nature—if only in meditation at first. Awareness promotes enlightenment and vibrational movement and this is the way of the future for those of us wanting to move forward.

These passages came to me via messages from the Light Beings, communicated from far outside the Earth. Therefore, their wish to "spread the word" that we need enlightenment and higher vibration is strong in this system. Know that each word not only applies to the situational questions you ask of your life now, but also points to concepts that we all need to master before we will be accepted into the worlds "out there."

I hope that this deck will become a small part of your growth, and I welcome you into my family circle in the stars.

Dinah Roseberry

BIBLIOGRAPHY

Gray-Cobb, Maiya. *The Numbers of Your Life*. Atglen, PA: Schiffer Publishing. 2012.
HubbleSite.org.
Javane, Faith. *Master Numbers: Cycles of Divine Order*. Atglen, PA: Schiffer Publishing. 1988.
Javane, Faith and Dusty Bunker. *Numerology and the Divine Triangle*. Atglen, PA: Schiffer Publishing. 1971.
Storm, Rayne. *In the Night Sky*. Atglen, PA: Schiffer Publishing. 2013.